GOD'S MESSENGER
A Collection of Poetry

VIOLA WASHINGTON

Tandem Light Press

Tandem Light Press
950 Herrington Rd.
Suite C128
Lawrenceville, GA 30044
www.tandemlightpress.com

Tandem Light Press paperback edition January 2016

ISBN: 978-0-9861660-6-8
Library of Congress Control Number: 2015944182

Biblical passages are from the King James Bible
Interior Design: WorldTech Graphics
Cover Design: Mary Gondolfo
Illustrations: TandemLight Illustrations

PRINTED IN THE UNITED STATES OF AMERICA

PERSONAL STATEMENT

God gave his gift of love to me so I could envision his works to see.
To write is an art, a special meaning to fill your heart with joy. At an
early age, I wrote poetry as a hobby, each time returning stronger than
before. Poetry is beauty deep in my soul. Through experience in life,
I'm pursuing that goal. Ministering through poetry to people, is God's
mission for me to do. It is a privilege and pleasure to share with you. My
strength, knowledge, and achievements come from God. I'm grateful.
Give Him the glory.

DEDICATION

To God, the Father, the Son, and the Holy Spirit, for making me your chosen vessel to write your anointed messages in your name. I am so honored and humbled.

To all my angels who were there for me, I love you. Michael, Michelle, Donna, and Alondo, my children, God bless you.

To my dear friends, Mary, Barbara, and Cassandra who were very supportive and encouraging to me. Love you all!

To Bishop Darrell and Angela Lewis, and also to the Family Community Fellowship Church. To God be the glory!

To Maya Angelou, who was a great inspiration to me and the gift God gave to me. Thank you so very much!

Praise God,
The Messenger!

CONTENTS

A TRIBUTE TO MY FATHER

From the rising of the sun
'Til the going down of the same
Giving honor, glory, and praise,
In Jesus' holy and righteous name

Thank you God, for creating the universe
Thanks for your beauty on planet earth
Thanks for your word seed planted on my heart
Faith, health, and strength, giving a new start

Thank you God, for your only begotten son
Who took all my sins through the holy one
Thank you Father, for the comforter you sent
Giving me understanding on how to repent

Thank you Jesus, for dying to myself
To keep you first before anyone else
We give you all the glory and praise
This is my tribute to you always

Thank you Lord, for your mercy and grace
That keeps me pressing on this earthly place
Without you Jesus, I'm a little zero,
To God be the glory, you are my hero!

A LOVE TREE

The tree of life with many branches
Spreading limbs in all directions;
Little, medium, and large ones too
Needing attention and protection.
Roots are where they first emerge
Birds and bees take advantage of what
they see,
The tree of life, a love tree.
A love tree is a tree of
Freedom,
With beautiful
blossoms in the air;
For April showers
bring spring flowers
More love is
everywhere,
With a special message for
us to see,
The tree of life, a love tree.

ANSWER THE CALL

A phrase was spoken in meditation
You listen and you hear
Yet you see no one at all
Who said that? Was it a ghost?
Fear not and answer the call

Can this be the Lord in me
Testing me to set me free
Let me know what I must do
Step by step to follow you

Rise up my child
And take your place
For I have given you
My favor and grace

In all that you do
Speak from your heart
Witness to others and
Make a brand new start

You haven't got a spirit of fear
Know that Jesus is always near
When you stumble or ever fall
I'll be the one to answer the call!

GOD'S MESSENGER

Preordained before my birth
To do great things here on earth
A seed was planted for my good
Speaking for God, he knew I would

Father teach and show me how
My purpose here to do
Please anoint me with your grace
And your power to take it through

As a child there was a passion
For writing poetry I didn't know
As the roots took place and grew
The harvest burst and then I knew

My purpose is humbling to God and me
To be used by him I couldn't see
Then all the pieces moved in place
He made me his messenger through Grace!

Now, I know my purpose on earth
Talking with God is always first
He will lead and help me to say
His anointed message, come what may!

I BELIEVE GOD!

Father God, this world is yours
And all that's within
You spoke and made everything
It's on you we depend

The holy trinity all in one
Father, Spirit, and only begotten Son
Blood, water and flesh
Thank you God, we are so blessed!

I believe through God's son
He gave his life to save us all
Through unbelief and disobedience
He allows us to stumble and fall

Our God waits patiently for us
To come around and in him trust
Sometimes we don't use good sense
That's why angels are our defense

I believe there's power in Jesus' name
When it comes, you're never the same
By Jesus' blood that cleansed our sin
That we may all enter in!

I believe God is coming back
His signs and wonders are right on track
Trucks, cars, buses, and trains
Tragedies happen over and over again

I believe God, going forth in him
To worship and praise the spirited realm
When you refuse and turn away
God gets victory from those who obey!

UNCONDITIONAL LOVE

Jesus loves me, this I know
For the Bible tells me so
Come to Jesus as you are
A true confession will take you far!

Jesus' love gives peace and joy
Reveals all truth and doesn't destroy
My faith and trust I have in Him
Depending on Jesus and not on them

Material things can't communicate
Or make me feel like Jesus can
Material things only imitate
The carnal love made by man

At the break of dawn, things can't tell
If I'm sick or when I'm well
At midnight when my oil runs low,
Things can't fix me up to go

When I'm hungry, things can't feed
Or even comfort when I'm in need
Only the love of Jesus can heal
For I know His love is real

Jesus loves me through thick and thin
He's closer to me than any friend
When I'm lonely, down, and out
He's always there without a doubt

I'd rather have Jesus more than anything
For the Bible tells me so
His unconditional love is part
Of what true love is in my heart!

BE YE THANKFUL

Thanking God is an honor to do
When He is first and leave out you
Thank God for Jesus and His blood
That saved and kept us from the flood

Thank you God for your Holy Spirit
Dwelling in us to lead the way
With mercy, grace, and faith in God,
Be ye thankful each and everyday

Thank God for life and keeping you here
His spirit you have, know no fear
So humble yourself and give God praise
Thank him for raising Jesus from the grave

Be thankful for Jesus, the mediator for us
Teaching God's word, in him we trust
Then showing us to love one another
That bonds us closer to each other

Thank God for his word seed and great work
Of prayer, worship, and testimonies too,
Thank God for angels and supplying our need
Be ye thankful for God's word, it will feed!

KNOW YOURSELF

Know yourself for who you are
A unique person of the universe
Travelling so fast in outer space
Racing to find your place

Your world is spinning round and round
Never knowing where you'll be
Take the time to realize
It starts inside of me

In the system, there is a flag
Of blue and white so clear
To warn you when there's trouble
Which no one likes to hear

Emotions seem to intensify
With feelings we can't identify
When we listen from the inside
There's always a solution
To welcome and accept the change
That makes a better constitution.

Editor's Choice Award Winner – 1994

LOOKING INSIDE

When I was a child I did not know
That things in life come and go
People were more important to me
Many lessons learned with eyes to see.

Sometimes I wanted to run and hide
The feelings of love I felt inside
A voice spoke out don't be that way
For I will help you every day.

I'll be with you when in distress
To give you joy and happiness
When I'm backed against the wall
He is my strength, my all and all.

As time passed by, I wondered why
I was hurt and confused, but strong and didn't cry
As a teenager, I traveled and explored
Reaching out with the help of the Lord.

Following the crowd was not for me
With an inner spirit I had to be free
Yes, I made mistakes, but God has forgiven
The force that made me tossed and driven.

I opened my heart so he could come in
To lead and guide and save me from sin
I keep pressing on and continue to pray
For soul salvation on Judgment Day.

THANK YOU GOD

Thank you God for creating me
From man's rib to reality
Oh God, thank you for sending your son
To do your will as you'd have it done

Thank you for saving a sinner like me
Now filled with the holy spirit-
Uplifted and made free,
Thank you, thank you God.

Thank you God for reaching out
To lift my burdens and all I care about-
You're always there to guide me through
The good and bad, for that I say thank you

Flawless perfected with compassion and love,
So peaceful and carefree like a flying dove.
Thank you for blessings you send from above.
Thank you, thank you God.

Thank you God for the gift to write
Your anointed message with spiritual insight
Thank you for your loving way
You keep in touch day by day.

Thank you God most of all,
For answering my prayers whenever I call.
It's toll free with an open line.
No holding and waiting just to talk anytime.

God is always there when we go to him in prayer
I tell him all my problems and he gives them special care
Thank God for who I am and all that I'm going to be-
To let my little light shine and keep walking close with thee.

Thank you God!

USE ME

Use me Lord, to your glory
To testify and tell the story
How you brought me all the way
Teaching me to watch and pray

Lifting up my self esteem
Shielding me from storms that rise
Brightening dark clouds beyond the skies
Use me, use me Lord

Direct my path when I stray
Keep me in the straight and narrow way
Fill my cup, then I will say
Use me, use me Lord

Fill me with the Holy Ghost
So I will trust you and obey
You are the potter and I am the clay
Use me, use me Lord

Our children today are hurting in school
For being misled and breaking rules
Joining gangs they know nothing of
Using drugs to contaminate their blood

They carry guns like one in authority
Taking lives into their own hands
Man cannot seem to make them understand
Corruption is rising all over the land

Jesus is speaking to the rich and poor,
Kings and queens more than ever before
The enemy is striving to take control
Call him a liar and salvage your soul

Those in politics, clean up your slates
Balance the scales and get things straight
Lawmakers and lawbreakers all in one
Hiding behind untruths you have done

If I can make a difference
To someone through your word
I say thank you Holy Spirit
What great message I have heard

Help me to see beyond the dream
Your reality of what it means
The works and miracles which I have seen
Use me, use me Lord

Acknowledged as one of the wor'ds most outstanding poem and poet
International Society of Poets, 1994

A SPIRITUAL AWAKENING

As I woke up one morning
My strength had gone away
I didn't know what to think
Or even what to say

As I struggled to my feet
The enemy made its play
In my realization
I fell on my knees to prey

My physical body was drained
From things I could not see
The spirit was aware of my need
I cried, Lord remember me

Lord God I am your child
I need you to get along
Touch me with your healing hand
Increase my faith and make me strong

The battle is not over
But help me safely through
To reach the other side
And finish your work I love to do

GOD IN CONTROL

Oh Lord how excellent is thy name
In heaven and all the earth,
With bright sunshine and rays of heat
Rain clouds we pray to burst.

Give God the praises for He's in control
Of all we do and say
If we have fallen short of your word
Forgive us Father this day.

The floods and heat remind us
Of your Bible stories we read,
How the Israelites suffered
When they would not take heed

Our greed for money and material things
Is not your way of life
Or worshiping idols and false prophets
Can only bring trouble and strife.

Master please help us if you will
To change our hearts and make us new,
To give you praise and all the glory
In everything we do.

"Thus says the Lord, the God of
hosts, the God of Israel; I have
spoken to them and they have not
listened, I have called to them
and they have not answered."
Jeremiah 35:17

Editor's Choice Award Winner - 1994

DEEP BLUES

Sometimes we call it depression
When we get quite upset
Feeling lost and so unloved
Turning within trying to forget

Who am I and what's my purpose
In life for me? Where is my place?
Is it in hiding with darkness I face,
Or on the streets with crime and waste?

Your faith has been shaken
By the deep blues man
Who comes to deceive and destroy
And keep you under his command

He comes to take your energy
Then program you under his control
It's a break up for you to make up
With your Lord for a higher goal

Believe in all positive things
Find your purpose to fulfil
Encourage others along the way
Then the blues in you will heal

DEFENSE ON THE CROSS

The Son of God was crucified
Then hung upon the cross
With tormentation He paid the price
So we would not be lost

They hung Him high
And stretched Him wide
To nail His hands and feet
Then pierced Him in His side
Which made the job complete

Oh how His precious blood ran down
So we could be free from sin
Then filled us with His Holy Spirit
That we could enter in

In agony, Jesus said forgive them
They know not what they do
I'm doing the will of my Father
And He will carry me through

Some thought the worst was over
When they buried Him in the grave
It was guarded day and night
So He would not leave their sight

While Jesus was in the ground,
Old Satan came hanging around
He had Him in his domain
But Jesus beat him at his own game

He took the keys to Hell, death and grave
And told Satan shut up, don't say another word
All power and authority was given to Me
The prophets and saints were all set free

Grave tried to hold Him, but up He came
Death had to let go, Power is His name
On the third day, the stone was rolled away
Jesus ascended into Heaven
To hear what His Father had to say

What about our cross
The ones we have to bear?
God, the Father, sent the Comforter
To let us know he's always there

A HEALING PRAYER

Touch us Lord with healing hands
Heal sisters and brothers all over the land
Heal our minds and cleanse our hearts
Bring us together, give us a new start

With heads bowed down on bended knees
Forgive us, kind Father, if you please
We're not worthy Lord, but we need a lesson
On learning to appreciate all our blessings

Hear our prayers as we turn to you
For self-understanding and mankind too
Anoint us kind Father that we might be
Meek and humble, yet worthy of thee

Lord God, you taught us not to go astray
By living through the word and praying all day
Lord, please stay with us and make our burdens light
Some still live in darkness and refuse to do right

Mold us and make us obedient to thee
Open our eyes that we might see
The good in others by looking within
And not just the surface or the color of skin

Touch us right now with your finger of Love
Send out your mighty power from Heaven above
I thank you Lord for your creation
Restore peace and harmony to all nations.

Amen

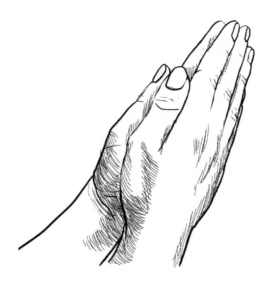

WINGS OF LOVE

Trust God in His wings of love
To take you on his flight
From all your fears and worry
Into Heaven's delight

A seat belt is never needed
With Him you are secure
Only when you trust Him
The more you will endure

It's peaceful in the wings of love
And joy that has no limit
With love flowing from your heart
And everything you put in it

So trust God's wings of love
To take you everywhere
Then pass his love to others
And let them know God cares

KEEP PRAYING

Keep on praying the Lord is nigh
Just keep praying He'll hear your cry,
He will dry your tears and answer you-
Trust in Him and He'll bring you through.

Keep on praying, Jesus is His name
Just keep praying, He'll heal your pain
He'll lift you up and put you down-
Just trust in Jesus and He'll bring you around.

Prayer is the key to the higher power
Keep on praying on your darkest hour
Faith is hope not seen, but it helps you bear-
Those heavy burdens, take it to God in prayer.

Keep on praying when you are accused
Just keep praying if you are abused,
God will fight your battles too-
Put your trust in him, there's nothing He won't do.

Keep on praying when things are going well
Pray about problems to no one else you'd tell
Just keep praying and stay on bended knee
My God will answer and give you victory.

THE HIDDEN PROMISE

There's a promise deep within me
It's something good yet very strange
With patience, this work of progress
Will surface itself from the grain

God has given me all that I need
In order to grow and achieve
Doing my part and knowing there's more
With an open heart, trusting Jesus to believe

When I don't give up on myself
Hope is not far off to see
By keeping focus on God the father
He will never give up on me

I am a work in progress
Every day is a season to pray
For God to reveal the inner glory
Of what I think, do and say

He promised to supply all my needs
He promised never to leave me alone
He promised peace, love and happiness
For my soul, in His heavenly home

THANK GOD FOR ANGELS

Thank you God for unseen angels
Assigned to watch over us
Day and night wherever we are
They are God's helpers from afar

Thank you god for sleep angels
Who watch us while we sleep
Thank you for your dreams
And all the visions we see
Thank you for traveling angels
Who help us reach our destiny

Thank you God for angels of love
When we feel so all alone
Thank you for your angels of peace
Bringing us blessings from your throne

Thank you for your angels of mercy
Helping us at work and play
Leading and guiding us all the way
Thank God for sending angels every day!

GOD'S WILL BE DONE!

When are we going to do God's will?
Our time, his time, no time
Ripping and running after things and money
Satan is rejoicing and making you funny

Your mind and body cannot rest
You have overworked it in the flesh
Some believe technology day and night
Instead of God's word that's always right

The protestors, media and crooks in crime
Fighting sex trafficking and towing the line
It's the antichrist, they do what he say
Instead of God's word, trust Him and obey

Watch and pray, time is winding down
Keep pressing on to get your crown
Game playing is over, God's will be done,
So we can go back with the Father and Son

THE MESSENGER

Dear Lord, please send us a message
One that will open the heart and mind
Anoint our ears so they will hear
Your teachings on living with mankind

Sometimes it's easy for us to give up
And not stay in Your Word
Speak Lord, speak, that we will live up
To Your laws which we have heard

The economy is sky high
No matter how hard we try
Tell us how and what to do
Let us hear directly from You

Going against Your will is wrong
So many suffer in the end
If we are weaker than we're strong
Strengthen us Lord, for we have sinned

Speak Lord, speak, hear us now
To God, the Father, we humbly bow
For repentance to You, that we'll be blessed
To live a Christian life in joy and happiness

ALL GLORY BELONGS TO GOD

From the beginning of time
And all in between
Give God the glory
For His beautiful works we have seen

From the rising of the sun
To the going down of the same
Give honor and glory
In Jesus' precious name

He's the unseen eye
That sits high and looks low
He watches and protects us
Everywhere we need to go

God supplies all our needs
In our hunger, he will feed
When we struggle in our test
Tired and weary, he gives rest

Doing His good work most of all
He won't forsake or let us fall
Give Him glory, He is our King
Give Him glory for everything!

GROWING SEEDS

A seed was planted long ago
Tucked deep within, waiting to grow
To spread its wings and soar in the wind
Gaining new heights in search of a friend.

With loving care from a gentle hand
Pray for strength to let it stand
Nurse it through puberty stage
Entering maturity that comes with age.

God's word is the ingredient
Depend on and enjoy
The treasure of His blessings
He has in store

The spirit is like a chamber in our hearts
To function without defects to destroy the
parts
Let go, let God be the source from above
Your seed will sprout up through His eternal
love

WHO ARE WE?

The Vine of life with many branches
Being processed from the inside out
Purging is needed to bring forth fruit
Then the buds begin to sprout

Some trimming and cutting must be done
Your nutrients and water comes from the Son!
A little discomfort and minimum pain
Your works and labor is not in vain

So reap your harvest from the true Vine
It's guaranteed you'll bear good fruit
Be Jesus' example, then you'll find
Your rewards will be greater
By leaving dead fruits behind!

FAMILY TIES

A strong family tie can set the tone
For bonding together and making a home
To love and share the good times in life
And deal with crisis when things are not right

Each member differs in a unique way
Striving for independence and new values today
Remembering our roots from the family tree
Increases the generation for pleasant memories

The strongest ties are families
In the blood line that we share
For families stay together
When they kneel to God in prayer

"Beloved, since God loves us so
Much, we also ought to love one
Another."
I John 4:11

SENIORS ON THE BATTLEFIELD

We take this time to honor our seniors,
For standing so very tall;
The ones who taught and set examples,
Preparing us for God's call.

For those who attended prayer meetings,
And sat on the mourner's bench;
For those who yielded not to temptation,
To make themselves content.

For those who prayed day and night,
We thank God for His unseen sight.
To those who testifies for us,
Thank you Lord, in Him you put your trust.

To those who have been mothers and fathers,
Not just to your children,
But relatives and many others,
With love, compassion, and dedication,
You planted seeds for manifestation.

Seniors stay on the Battlefield
Pray on 'till the Lord says stop;
There's plenty of work to be done,
Every generation is a brand new crop.

When you feel you're no longer needed,
Stand in the gap for those who don't know.
Somewhere along life's journey,
Appreciation to you they will show.

You may not be here,
When the good comes back to you.
Yet you'll know within your heart
You did the best that you could do.

So seniors march on God's battlefield
Step and raise his banner high
You have the ammunition of wisdom
To extinguish the enemies' spark of fire

Seniors, you must lead the way
Help train up our children
Show them around the pitfalls and mountains
To thirst for the blood of Jesus' fountain.

Strive on with faith and courage
Until God gives you the command
To enter into his golden gates
And enjoy his heavenly land.

TOGETHERNESS

In the beginning, God created the heaven and the earth
But the earth was without form
The spirit of God moved upon the waters
And a beautiful creation was born

Light, darkness, grass, and a fruit tree
Two great nights for night and day
The stars were set in heaven
To rule over the earth, Genesis say

With all power in his hand
God continued creating his master plan
Every living creature came into existence
Including woman and man

Everything he made was blessed and good
Be ye fruitful and multiply
Something was missing without a sound
Man was made from dust of the ground

Later came Eve from Adam's ribs
Both were blessed with happiness
As long as they obeyed
Something took place, so they stayed
To face the consequences together

Through God's children and his jobs
Our heavenly father is speaking today
Signs of the season are here for a reason
For His message He's trying to convey

Who suffered and died on the cross for us
Yet we continue to bicker and fuss
Over everything out of our control
Instead of coming together for a higher goal

Was Jesus death all in vain
Or have we lost sight of salvation to gain
When will we learn a better way
For solving our problems and going astray

Let our steps be established
When you ponder the path of your feet
Then with guidance and divine direction
You'll see beyond the clouds you meet

Watch for the rainbow in the sky
It's a sign that all is clear
With wisdom and misunderstanding
We can press on and persevere

It's amazing that we can accomplish
When we come together and share
Much joy abounds with happiness
Like magic, that's called togetherness

Our time is slowly running out
For all nations to come together
We as a people need to change
Before we enter God's kingdom in heaven

There will be no separation
From one race to another
It will be one big celebration
For all God's Christian generation

Let us move forward before it's too late
Repent in Jesus' name and cooperate
Faith with courage can open the door
Believe all things will come together
And unity will reign forever more

GOD'S TRUTH IS MARCHING ON

Rumors of wars are all across the land
Heads of nations don't know what to do
The wealthy and rich are still making deals
Using the poor and going against God's will

The bargaining table is just a ploy
To obtain advantage over opponents to destroy
When things backfire, they call a name
But no one wants to take the blame

Stumbling blocks are pushed in place
Determined to divide the human race
Rocks cry out but they don't hear
They try to hide and live in fear

The children cry day and night
While mommy and daddy fuss and fight
How can they learn to give respect
With the bad example some parents set

No morals or guidelines to follow behind
It's a losing battle, but there's still time
Use the power that was given to you
Which no one can take or even sue

Stand up for justice
And fight with your head
Break down Satan's defense
Choose God instead

Let him lead and guide you along
With faith and strength to make you strong
Humble yourself to his will and way
The choice is yours, choose God today!

STREET PEOPLE

Street people live one day at a time,
Looking for shelter while exposed to crime,
Some look in darkness while others seek the light
Trying to survive and do what is right

Much like a fisherman who pulls in his net,
They congregate together for a long night rest
Put yourself in their shoes
Oh how you'd wonder, "what must I do?"

Sisters and brothers, we must help others
To turn to God and not give up,
To supply our needs and fill our cup,
To find his way when we are lost,
Or pay the price at any cost
To trust and believe, then we will receive-
Joy in our hearts like never before
And talk with Jesus when he knocks at the door.

God's shelter is for all who wish to abide
Just open your heart and let Him come inside,
There's no deposit or rent to pay,
Follow His commandments and walk His way.

Go tell the people about this great man
How He made the whole world with His hands
The hungry were fed and the sick were healed
He'll do it well, if only we yield.

The mute began to talk
The lame was made to walk
The blind man was made to see
What he thought would never be.

The deaf was made to hear
Jesus drew all of them near
And said, I am the way, the truth, and the light
Just follow me, it's going to be alright.

Lean to my understanding and not of your own
I won't forsake you or ever leave you alone
I go to prepare a place for you
At my father's house, you are welcome too.

Praise God

DISCIPLESHIP 2000

Automation is a temporary replacement
That's designed to process and control
It's a self-serving idol of destruction
Without a heart, mind, or soul

Man is anxious for advancement
Toward a future he's trying to reach
How far can he go or even stand
Discipleship 2000 is not in command

When the system backs up
And the mechanisms break down
They push emergency power
Because man cannot be found

Come in, come in, disciple 2000
What must we do now?
We have a problem with the internet
We need a contact, show us how

Just imagine how far we would get
The kingdom of heaven is at hand
Discipleship 2000 could never fit
Into the Master's plan

The discipleship of Jesus
Was equipped very well
Their teacher had all power
And commanded them to excel

The disciples were sent to lost sheep
To preach, heal the sick, and raise the dead
There was no static or interference
They pressed on and moved ahead

This is what the Master expects
From Christians who walk his way
To follow all his teachings
Not man's that leads you astray

Automatic controls will corrupt your mind
They steer you from the main line
Contentment kicks in and takes the place
Of life and reality we refuse to face

No strings or buttons to pull and push
Our Father works day and night for us
All He asks is to follow him
Only believe and in Him only trust

It's never too late to turn around
And plant our feet on solid ground
When we throw the anchor out
The old ship of Zion will stop and shout
For all that enter and come on board
We give the highest praise to Christ our Lord.

So the body of Christ must get right
For the kingdom of heaven is at hand
Discipleship 2000 will never fit
Eternally into the Master's plan.

GET ON BOARD!

Get on board, it's never too late
God needs all to participate
Jesus gave his life for you and me
His plans are larger than we can see

By loving God first,
Then self and all others,
We can communicate together
With our sisters and brothers

Feed the hungry and hurting ones
Like our father did through His son
Serve them with compassion and love
Many blessings will fall from above

We were called for his good works
For his purpose and his grace
Let us practice what we have learned
And continue to seek his face

God gave us all his gifts
To use for his honor and glory
To demonstrate and to witness
Then share and spread the gospel story!

ALL TORE UP!

In my head I was tore up
From the floor up
And I don't even drink
It messed up my mind
So I couldn't even think

No matter what I tried
It played hard ball inside
When I called on my friend
Jesus jumped right on in

They played two to three innings
That was just the beginning
Of Satan's tempting test for me
Oh, but Jesus will heal and set free

Stubborn Satan won't give up
Forgetting Jesus drank that bitter cup
Clouds in the sky heavy and low
When Jesus spoke they had to go!

I kept calling on that name
On my pillow I dug in deep
Jesus commanded the pain to leave
And put me right to sleep!

YOU'RE NOT ALONE

Let not your heart be troubled
And your mind begin to roam
God knows your every thought
He's right there, you're not alone

Tell Jesus all about it
He's waiting just to hear
Your fears and your anxieties
He will comfort and draw you near

Ask Jesus to touch with healing hands
Clear your mind to understand
He loves you daughter, don't forget
God is not through with you yet

Ask for patience, he'll give that too
Grace and mercy will see you through
Keep looking up to the father above
He just keeps sending LOVE, LOVE, LOVE

Jesus is Love

VICTORY IN THE WILDERNESS

Don't let the wilderness suck you in
The power of Jesus is your friend
Call on him, yes, that name
Not those things, your fortune and fame.

For they will be sucked in quick sand too
You can speak but they won't know to do
God wants more praise so raise your hands
He'll bring you out to the promise land

The wilderness is a desolate barren ground
It's like quick sand, you slowly drown
With God, and a born again Degree!
Nothing is impossible when you believe!

Remember God in your wilderness
Repent, rejoice for righteousness
It's your turn to be happy and blest
Praise God in and out of your wilderness

MAKE ME WHOLE

Thank you Lord for this day
Have mercy on me when I stray
Help me back where I belong
Send your power and make me strong

Sometimes the quicksand of the flesh
Hinders me, then I'm not blessed
But in my spirit it takes control
And arise like the sun,
From the depth of my soul

Crying out, O God, help me
Fill your purpose predestined to be
For I am willing to do your will
In the name of Jesus, I honestly appeal

Without the anointing,
Your work is in vain
Lift me up higher
To give praise in Jesus' name
Amen

SHOWERS OF BLESSINGS

Showers of blessings
Saturate God's earth
With much needed water
To spring forth new birth

Animals, trees, and bees,
Flowers, insects, and seeds
For farmers to plant and reap
Fresh air to breathe in deep

Human beings with jobs
To work and to live
Soften our hearts, Lord
To love and forgive

Showers of blessings fall on us
Only when God's light will shine
Restore our hearts and minds anew
Oh God, just one more time!
Amen!

GOD'S LIGHT LIVES IN US!

Let your light shine
For all the sinners to see
Share what God's done
For you and me

He brought us out of darkness
Into his marvelous light
To teach us about his love
And make everything alright

We are God's chosen people
Set apart for his good works
To show a mixed up people
God's not last; he's always first

He's the holy trinity, three in one
The Father, Spirit, and only begotten Son
Get thee behind, Satan
He's our source of all we need
It is written; the word of God will feed!

THERE'S ONLY ONE DOOR!

Come, come while there's still time
Leaving everything else behind
Robbers are coming to steal, kill, and destroy
Leading you to hell forevermore

No warnings at all
It will be taken by force
Try Jesus' way and you'll be alright
My yoke is easy and my burden is light

For I am the way, the truth, and life
Learn of me, hear and know my voice
Come, come now, there's only one door
You are welcome, make Jesus your choice!
Help me Lord to make this plain
It's only your power in Jesus name

RESTORING DEAD SPIRITS!

Dead spirits live right here on earth
They dishonor God by doing other things first
That's not the way it's supposed to be
Read Ezekiel and set your spirit free

All this destruction is His plans
Why? Because we disobey His commands
From east to west, and north to south,
God is spewing His wrath out of His mouth

God's chosen leaders are doing their best
To teach and preach the word of righteousness
The warnings keep coming yet you don't hear
You obey the flesh and live in fear

Life is in the Spirit
And it lives in the Light
So come out of darkness
Leave the wrong and turn to right

Turn and repent from death to life
We need you Lord to deliver us from strife
Breathe on us Jesus like never before
So we can cast those demons out to shore!

Please, please, Father hear our plea
Give us another chance for eternity
Revive our hearts and minds anew
So we can live a Christian life for you
Amen!

MOVING FREELY

No more chains for us today
Quality time with Jesus keeps them away
Wars are raging slowly but sure
Get in God's army and become secure

We must move forward to finish the race
Existing up from this earthly place
Good works done, principalities won
To God be the glory, for Jesus, His Son!

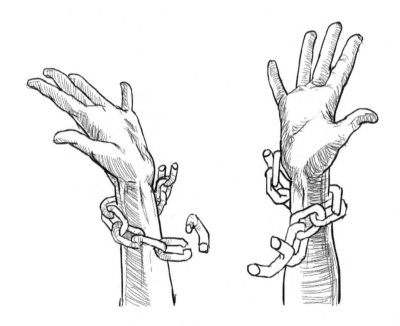

FLYING WITH JESUS

While on my flight up in the air
I called on Jesus and he was there
Flying high up over the clouds
It was quiet and never loud.

Your beauty God, is an awesome sight
Flying the skies day or night,
Up, up, and away over cities and towns
Your guardian angels were all around.

Preparing the plane for it to land,
You guided it with your gentle hand.
The runway was a little rough
My trip was safe and that's enough.

Thank you Lord for a safe air flight
Thanks again for making everything right.
I thank you for keeping me in your care
And never failing to answer my prayer.

Amen

GOD'S BEAUTY QUEEN

Someday I'm going to be a queen
The one God would have me be
Pretty gowns, jewels, crown and all
When he gets through processing me

When I stand before the mirror
And look inside of myself
The inner beauty of Jesus
Will flow to everyone else

I'll thank him in the morning
For the beauty queen I've become
Again at noon I'll thank him
For the prayer queen he has won

As the sun is going down
I'll praise him with all my heart
That God's beauty keeps on glowing
And his love will never depart

HANGING OUT WITH JESUS!

God uses ordinary people
To hang out with Him you know
Those who don't mind traveling
The round about ways he goes

It's alright to be in the valley
It's alright when there's doubt
But when we trust and hang with Jesus,
He will surely bring us out

Someone asked, where are we going Jesus?
And he replied, to the mountain top
Oh my, will it take a long time?
Do as I say, then you'll be fine

The road is tough and hard to climb
All obstacles will disappear
Have no fear, the Son of God is here
To carry us through and draw us near

We must go to the mountain top
And talk to the Father for ourselves
God will use you, then tell you what to do
To be a good example for someone else

While you're in the pruning stage
There's a cleansing that must be done
Your system has carried old garbage for days
Next comes the process from the Holy One

Can you think of a better place
Than to hang out at the mountain top?
You have to make visits everyday
Or down in the valley you will drop

God will make a nobody into somebody
That will teach the people his ways,
Who can be a leader in doing God's will,
And will give Him all the praise

THE PRIZE

Bless the Lord, oh my soul, and all that's within me
Stay by my side, lead and guide me there to defend thee
The map of life with hills and mountains to climb
Listening to instructions, your way we'll surely find.

Teach us to keep our eyes in front and minds opened wide
As we travel down the road racing for the prize
The lanes are like miles on a highway, they never seem to end-
Hold on to faith, stop and rest, refuel and start again.

Endurance is a virtue with patience to overcome-
With removal of obstacles that obstruct your race to run.
Watch out for yield and cautions signs
They are for safety to keep you in line.

When in doubt with a feeling of dismay,
It's part of your trial, keep pressing on God's way
In a spiritual race, there are rewards too
Only if you are willing to stay in and follow through.

Mixed forces signal conflict at the intersections
Rejuvenate your energy, then follow all directions
Don't be distracted by those in disguise
Look to the front until you reach the prize.

A GOD FEARING SERVANT!

A spirit born, a spirit mourned
But now wades out to shore
To spread its wings and soar above
For Jesus loved me more.

Made in God's image as a woman
To find her place on earth
A wonderful journey to explore
But Jesus loves me more

My life began to change for good
From trials and tribulation in the hood
The old woman feel the new emerged
God gave a mission, for him I served.

Maya Angelou rest in peace
A God fearing woman now released
Your legacy you left behind
Will comfort many in dark times

Your spirit will always linger here
To encourage others far and near
Bringing out the best in you and me
To pass on the anchor for others to see

We must press on and not drop out
Giving glory, praise, and a victory shout
While staying in the Christian race
Becoming a conqueror through God's grace

Let your light shine and serve the Lord
With all your heart like never before
Until we meet, I love you all
But Jesus loved me more!

BIRTHDAY GREETINGS, PASTOR LEWIS!

Pastor Lewis, I appreciate you
For all the things you say and do
I discerned the light of Christ from within
With confirmation, I found a good friend

You emerged from the nest
To become your better best
A divine intervention came from on high
You stretched forth your wings and began to fly

You remind me of Jesus and his humbleness
Your obedience and perseverance for righteousness
You are our earthly shepherd and we, the sheep
Your teachings of God's word is simple and deep

I admire the way you break it down
For those who see the surface of ground
Of course, with your personal testimony
They can relate and not feel lonely

When God knows your mind and heart
Just like the special seed he planted
With your anointing and understanding
You are committed and take nothing for granted

God's will is to soar like an eagle
All over his beautiful universe
Until you come full circle
With all eagles to break the curse!

I see you, Pastor Lewis, just moving us
Like Jesus did with power and gusts
You will be rewarded when your time comes
Praise God, the Father, Holy Spirit, and Son!

Give God The Glory

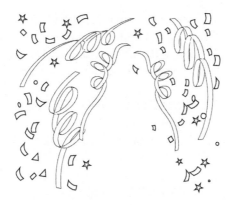

AN EAGLET IN TRAINING

A seed emerged seven years ago
No one knew how fast it would grow
Only the creator who made the seed
Watered, nourished, and supplied its need

It started down in the valley
With a blind and foolish foundation
Through faith, prayer, and good works,
It has become a great Christian nation

Dist. Elder Lewis, walk on by faith
And not by your eyesight
Trusting and believing that
All things will be alright

Mistakes will be made
While teaching you a lesson
On how to trust God
For all of your blessings

Now you are an Eaglet in training
Wearing a black crown while you're reigning
Congratulations, and soar on in space
It came to pass through God's grace

You'll be taken out of your nest
Then tested to do your very best
Attacks will come from you know who
It is finished, press on and follow through

Keep on soaring higher and higher
Stay focused and humble even when you stumble
In doing good works for God's people
That's how you become a large eagle!

You made it, Amen!

THE MARRED LOST SON!
STILL IN GOD'S HAND

When you're out in the world,
You can only go so far
It will lead you around in circles
And you don't know where you are
You mind and health begin to decline
Food and medicine, you cannot find
Wondering in the wilderness until you fall
Becoming homeless with no one to call
When prayers are still going up for you
Angels are watching and protecting too
My Father from heaven above
Touched you with his finger of love
God led you to a place for help
You were very much outside of yourself
Slowly, you began to come around
And found yourself in another town
Where and how did I get here?
God put you to sleep and drew you near!
So he could restore your mind and heart
You'll be a testimony for a brand new start!

Was Lost, Now Found!!!

GOING BACK TO GOD!

America, America, open your eyes and ears
Repent, pray for God to remove all your fears
We turned away from the real leader
And started following a fake deceiver

Our minds, hearts, and souls
Were turned away from God's goals
He keeps speaking to all of us
We gave up "In God we trust"

We are not being fruitful, dead like a fig tree
Stuck in bondage, chains, and captivity
God brought us out once and he'll do it again
Through the blood of Jesus that cleansed our sin

Alba, Father, which art in heaven,
Please give us a chance to come back to you
To complete your journey given for us to do
With grace and mercy to see us through

America, America, keep praying and stand
So God can give us back our freedom and land
We humble ourselves unto you this day
Then put our trust in you, God, to obey!

Now we are soldiers in God's army,
Marching and praying toward our destiny
The battle is yours, Lord have your way
We believe and trust in your word today

Thank You, God, for grace and restoration
For your blood stained banner under one nation
America, America, we must do it God's way
By humbling ourselves and pray, pray, pray

Amen, Amen, Amen!

ABOUT THE AUTHOR

Reverend Viola Washington is a God-fearing servant. She is a saved, called, anointed Christian of Jesus Christ born in the nation's Capital, Washington, DC. She is a member of Family Community Fellowship Church under Bishop Darrell Lewis.

Her children have played a major role in Reverend Washington's life, and very much so today. She has had a deep love for babies and seniors since she was a little girl. Through the grace of God, she has a purpose and is doing God's will with His help. She says, "To God be the glory for the awards and achievements He has allowed her to receive." She is very grateful because it is all about Jesus. The Reverend asks that we all pray for her in Jesus' name!